To:
From:
Message:

Praying the Names of God

© 2018
First edition 2018 Christian Art Publishers
PO Box 1599, Vereeniging, 1930, RSA

Designed by Christian Art Publishers

Images used under license from Shutterstock.com

Printed in China

ISBN 978-1-4321-2727-5

19 20 21 22 23 24 25 26 27 28 – 13 12 11 10 9 8 7 6 5 4

Praying
THE NAMES
of God

CHRISTIAN ART
PUBLISHERS

Psalm 23

The Lord is my shepherd;
I have everything I need.
He lets me rest in green pastures.
He leads me to calm water.
He gives me new strength.
He leads me on paths that are right
for the good of His name.
Even if I walk through a very dark valley,
I will not be afraid, because You are with me.
Your rod and Your shepherd's staff comfort me.
You prepare a meal for me in front of my enemies.
You pour oil of blessing on my head;
You fill my cup to overflowing.
Surely Your goodness and love will be with me
all my life,
and I will live in the house of the Lord forever.

THE GOOD SHEPHERD

Poimen Kalos

*"I am the good shepherd.
The good shepherd lays down
His life for the sheep."*

JOHN 10:11

Lord, You search for me and keep me
like a shepherd tends his sheep.
Thank You for always giving me
another chance to return to You
when I wander off like a lost sheep.

Amen.

Mighty Creator

Elohim

This name means "Strength" or "Power." God is transcendent, mighty and strong. *Elohim* is the great name of God, displaying His supreme power, sovereignty, and faithfulness in His covenant relationship with us.

In the beginning God created
the heavens and the earth.

Genesis 1:1

We also pray the name *Elohim* as our strong tower when we seek refuge. That is the name Proverbs 18:10 uses. It says, "The name of the LORD (*Elohim*) is a fortified tower; the righteous run to it and are safe."

Mighty God, You created everything
out of nothing. Help me to know
You as the one true God –
the Creator of heaven and earth.
Amen.

The name of God is His Being,
not as He is in Himself,
but as He is revealed to us.

Herman Hoeksema

God Has a Great Plan for You

You are *loved*.

You are *wonderfully made*.

You are *beautiful*.

You have *purpose*.

You are a *masterpiece*.

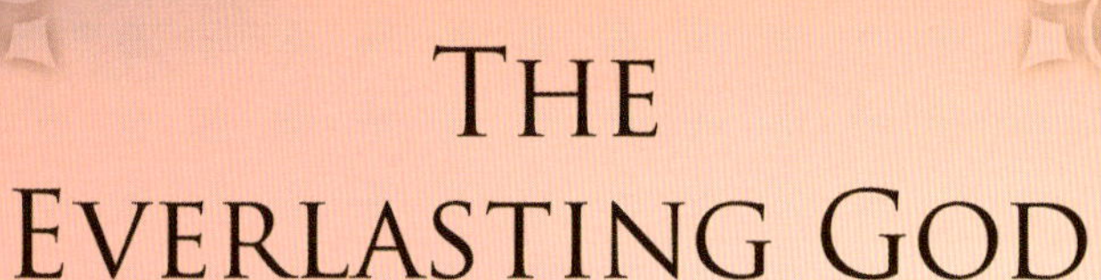

The Everlasting God

El Olam

God has no beginning and no end. His plans stand firm forever. And His plans are to give you a future filled with hope.

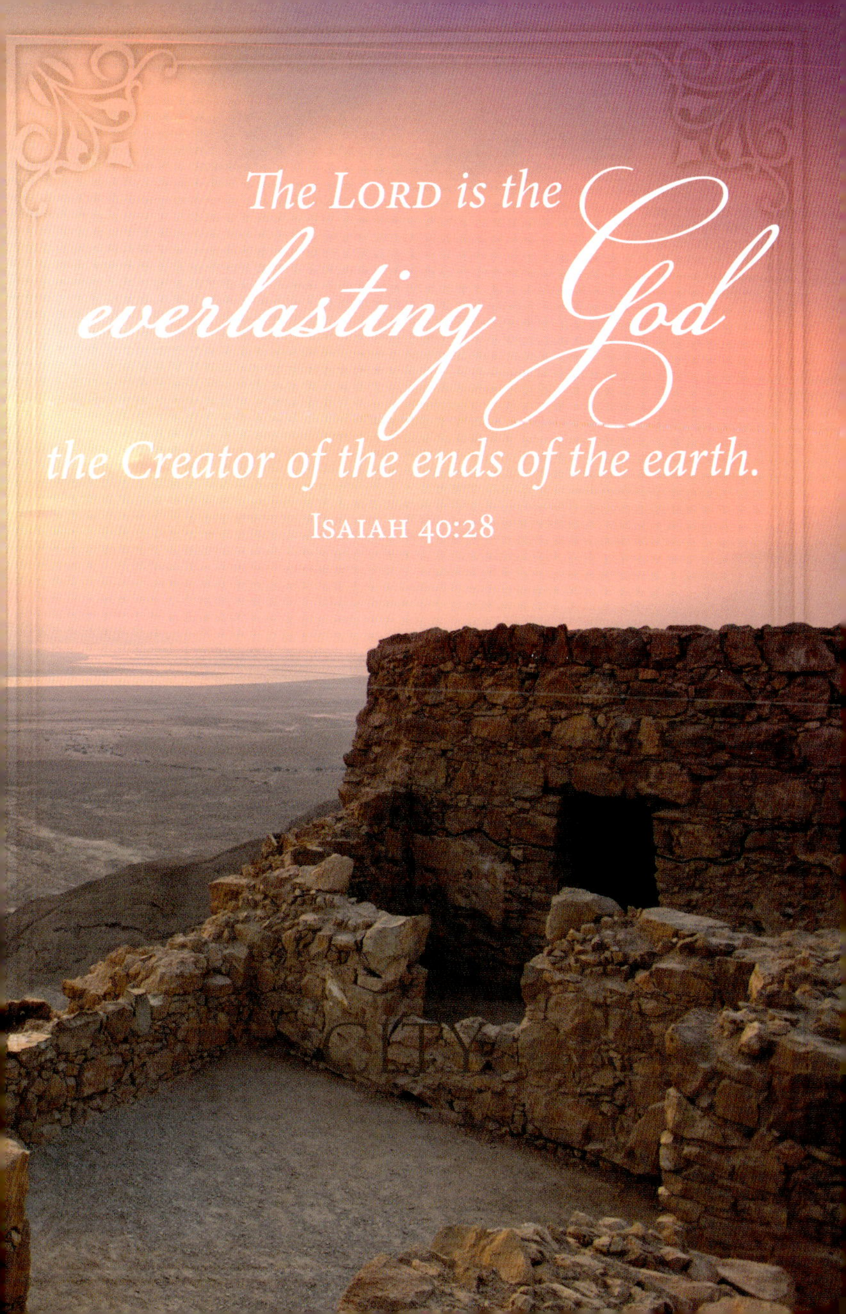
The LORD is the
everlasting God
the Creator of the ends of the earth.
ISAIAH 40:28

THE LORD

Adonay

This word *Adonay* referring to the Lord appears more than three hundred times in the Hebrew Scriptures. Pray to *Adonay*, and tell Him that you long to surrender your life completely to Him. Only He can make you able to fulfill your life's purpose.

Lord, I need You ...

You are my Lord;
apart from You
I have no good thing.

Psalm 16:2

The God Who Sees Me

El Roi

"You are the God who sees me."
Genesis 16:13

Lord, You know everything about me.
You know when I sit and when I rise.
Help me to fix my eyes on You,
and to trust Your vision for my life.
Amen.

THE LAMB OF GOD

Arnion

"Look, the Lamb of God,
who takes away the sin of the world!"
JOHN 1:29

Lamb of God,
I praise and glorify You
for taking the sins of the world
on Your shoulders. You were
slain for our transgressions.
Amen.

There is no one holy like the Lord;
there is no one besides You;
there is no Rock like our God.
1 Samuel 2:2

The Lord My Rock

Yahweh Tsuri

"The Lord is my rock, my fortress
and my deliverer; my God is my rock,
in whom I take refuge, my shield and
the horn of my salvation. He is my stronghold,
my refuge and my Savior – from violent people
You save me. "I called to the Lord,
who is worthy of praise, and
have been saved from my enemies."

2 Samuel 22:2-4

The Hebrew word for peace, *shalom*, means wholeness in all of life, completeness, welfare, safety. God is our source of all of these blessings.

"When you pass through the waters,
I will be with you;
and when you pass through the rivers,
they will not sweep over you."
Isaiah 43:2

Peace

Yahweh Shalom

Lord, I long for peace that
only You can give.
Help me to wait patiently
for Your *shalom*.
Amen.

"I am the Lord*,*
and I do not change."

Malachi 3:6

THE LION OF THE TRIBE OF JUDAH

Leon ek tes Phyles Iouda

Jesus is the Lion of Judah (Rev. 5:5)
and the Lamb of God (Rev. 5:6) –
He was lionhearted and lamblike, strong
and meek, tough and tender, aggressive
and responsive, bold and brokenhearted.
He sets the pattern for manhood.

JOHN PIPER

My Refuge

I will say of the Lord, *"He is my refuge and my fortress, my God, in whom I trust."*
Psalm 91:2

God, be my strong fortress.
I will sing praises to You,
my safe Refuge from the storms of life.
I trust in Your wonderful name.
Amen.

God is our refuge and strength,
an ever-present help in trouble.
Therefore we will not fear,
though the earth give way
and the mountains fall into the heart of the sea,
though its waters roar and foam
and the mountains quake with their surging.

PSALM 46:1-3

He Is Always with You

The Lord replied,
"My Presence will go with you,
and I will give you rest."
Exodus 33:14

Lord, I trust in You to do
what no one else can do,
in ways that no one else can work,
doing the wonders no one
else can perform.
Amen.

It often takes
the darkness of a storm
to show us the light
of God's presence.

Tony Evans

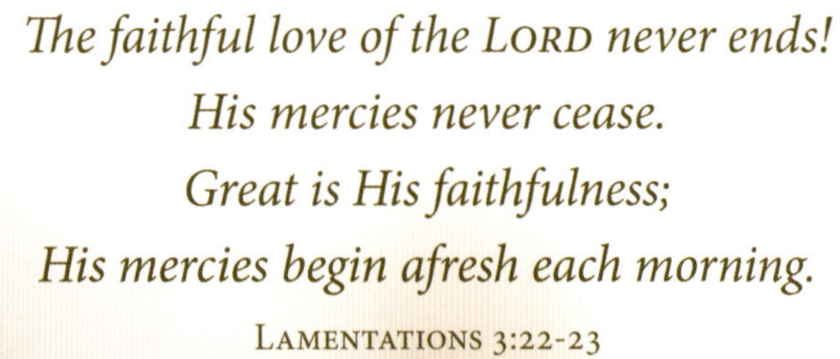

The faithful love of the Lord never ends!
His mercies never cease.
Great is His faithfulness;
His mercies begin afresh each morning.

Lamentations 3:22-23

THE LORD WILL PROVIDE

Yahweh Yireh

The compound name of God, *Yahweh Yireh* is first mentioned in Genesis 22:14. "YIREH" means to "see" or to "provide" or to "foresee" as a prophet.

When you pray to *Yahweh Yireh*, you pray to the God who knows everything. He sees the future, the past and the present. Therefore He can provide in your every need, because He knows everything about your life.

So Abraham called that place
The Lord Will Provide.
And to this day it is said, "On the mountain of the Lord it will be provided."

Genesis 22:14

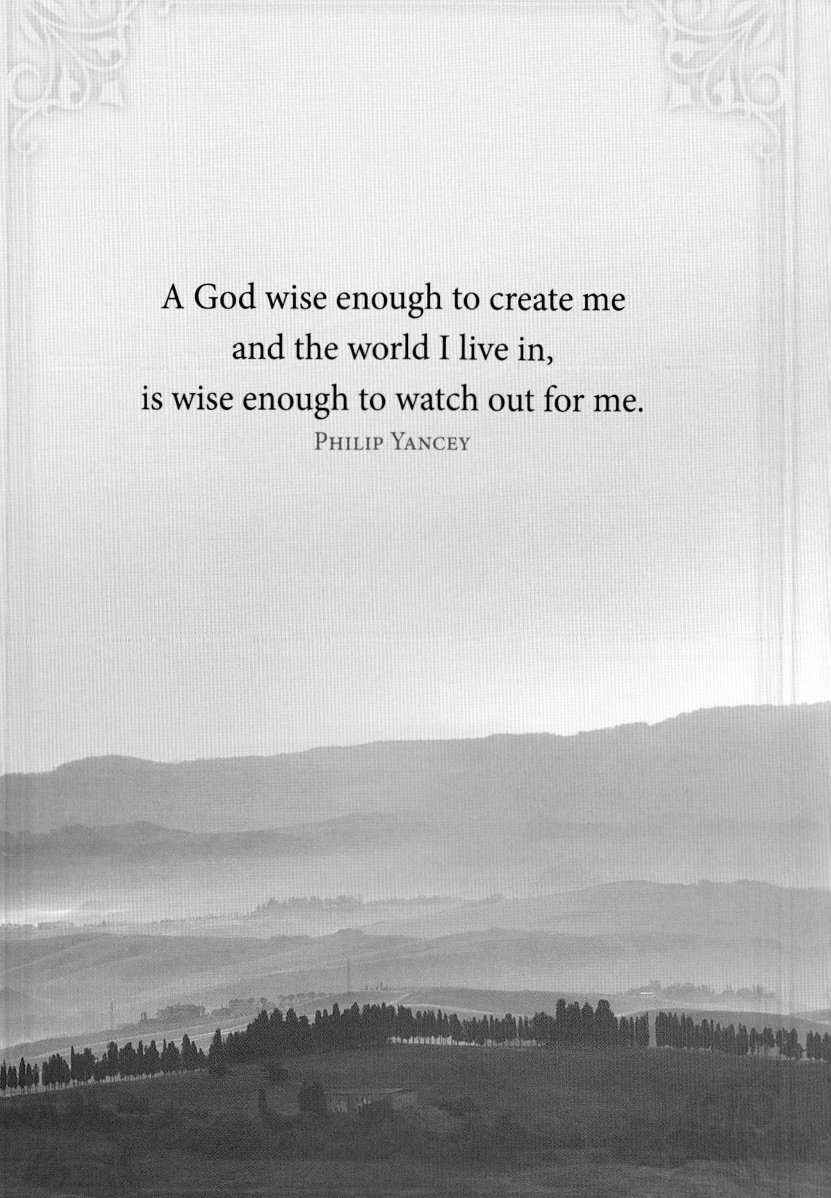

A God wise enough to create me
and the world I live in,
is wise enough to watch out for me.

Philip Yancey

GOD ALMIGHTY

El Shadday

This name means "God Almighty," the God who is all-sufficient and all-bountiful, the source of all blessings.

The Lord Is My Banner

Yahweh-Nissi

Moses built an altar there and named it Yahweh-Nissi (which means "the Lord is my banner").
Exodus 17:15

Today, as you face the spiritual battles here on earth, remember that the Lord gives us the victory. Hold high the banner of His strength, peace and love.

God is Infinite

God is beyond measure – we cannot define Him by proportions or magnitude. He has no beginning, no end, and no limits.

Oh, the depth of the riches of the wisdom and knowledge of God! How unsearchable His judgments, and His paths beyond tracing out!

Romans 11:33

The name *Emmanuel* takes in the whole mystery. Jesus is "God with us." He had a nature like our own in all things, sin only excepted. But though Jesus was "with us" in human flesh and blood, He was at the same time very God.

J. C. Ryle

The Bread of Life
JOHN 6:35

The Light of the World
JOHN 8:12

The Resurrection and the Life
JOHN 11:25

The Way and the Truth and the Life
JOHN 14:6

The True Vine
JOHN 15:1

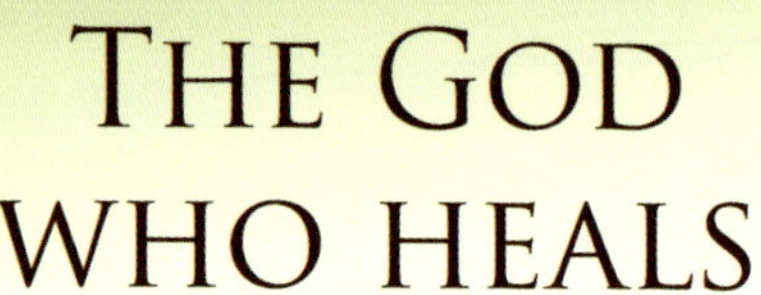

THE GOD WHO HEALS

Jehovah Rophe

The God who heals. He is the remedy for mankind's brokenness through His Son, Jesus Christ.

We need to *find God*,

and He cannot be found

in noise and restlessness.

God is the *friend of silence*.

See how nature – trees, flowers,

grass – *grows in silence*;

see the stars, the moon and the sun,

how they *move in silence* …

We need *silence* to be

able *to touch souls*.

MOTHER TERESA

THE LORD OUR RIGHTEOUSNESS

Yahweh Tsidkenu

You are the Righteous Judge.
Be merciful and gracious towards me,
and help me not to judge others,
but to rather pray for them.
Amen.

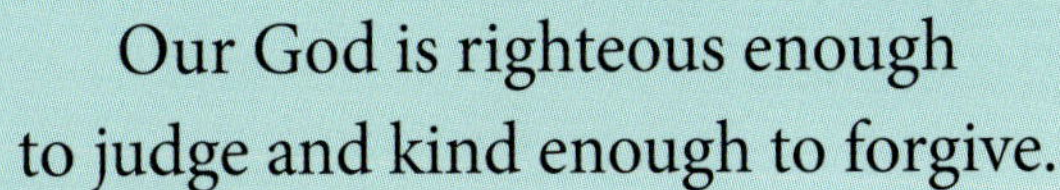

Our God is righteous enough
to judge and kind enough to forgive.

Kevin DeYoung

"And this will be His name:
'The Lord *Is Our Righteousness.'*
In that day Judah will be saved,
and Israel will live in safety."

Jeremiah 23:6

For the Lord *your God is*
living among you.
He is a mighty savior.
He will take delight in you with gladness.
With His love, He will calm all your fears.
He will rejoice over you with joyful songs.

Zephaniah 3:17

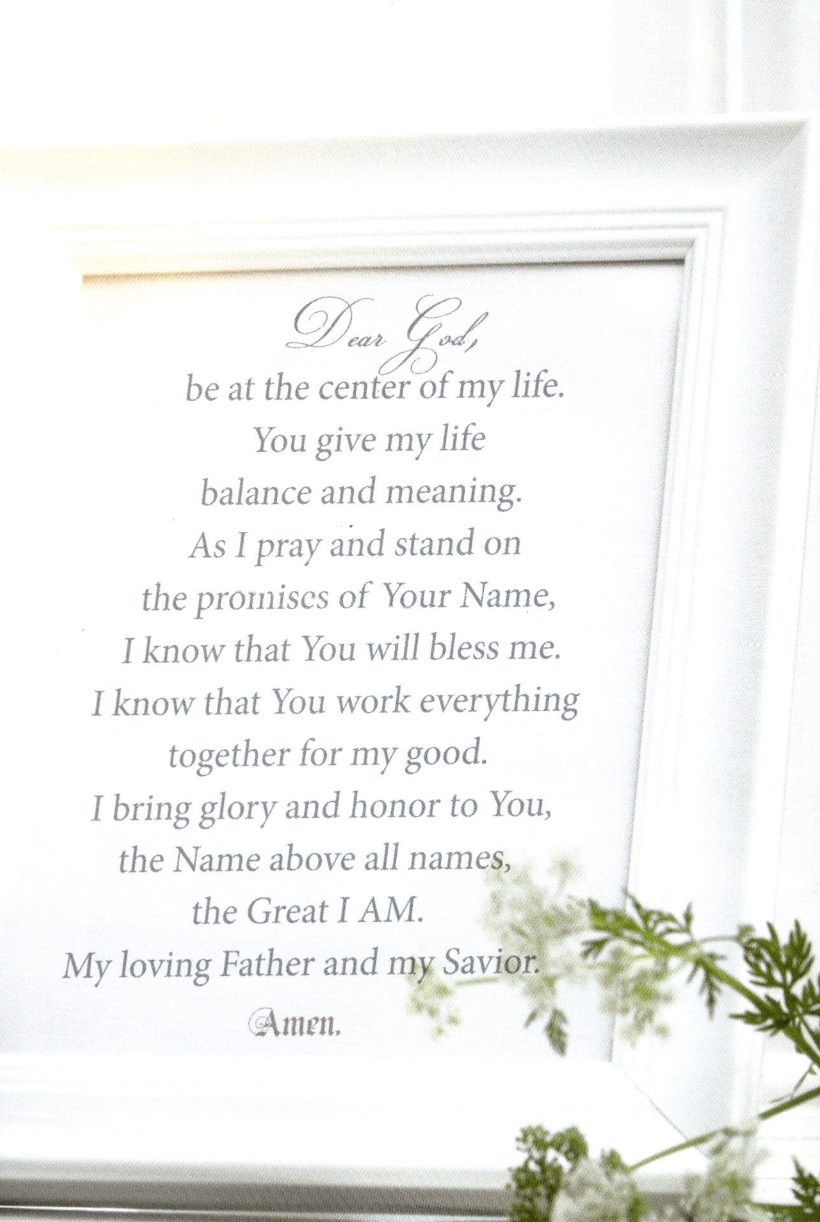
Dear God,
be at the center of my life.
You give my life
balance and meaning.
As I pray and stand on
the promises of Your Name,
I know that You will bless me.
I know that You work everything
together for my good.
I bring glory and honor to You,
the Name above all names,
the Great I AM.
My loving Father and my Savior.
Amen.

"I am the Alpha and the Omega," says the Lord God, "who is, and who was, and who is to come, the Almighty."
REVELATION 1:8

Alpha and omega are the first and last letters of the Greek alphabet. From an alphabet you make words, and Jesus Christ is called the "Word of God".

The only language God speaks and understands is the language where Jesus is the Alpha and the Omega and all the letters in between.

The Alpha
and
The Omega

Truth

God is the source of all truth. Our God, who is present everywhere and knows all things, has total understanding of what is real, what is right, and what is true. Whatever He promises will always be fulfilled.

God's *truth* frees us
to live as He intended.

"You will know the truth,
and the truth
will set you free."

John 8:32

FATHER

"Our Father in heaven,
hallowed be Your name."
MATTHEW 6:9

Father, thank You for showing us
what real Fatherly love looks like.
Strengthen my identity as Your child.
I want to glorify Your name
by mirroring You to others.
Amen.

"For the Lamb
at the center of the throne
will be their shepherd;
'He will lead them to
springs of living water.'
'And God will wipe away
every tear from their eyes.'"
REVELATION 7:17